ROMANTIC
PRAIRIE STYLE

ROMANTIC
PRAIRIE STYLE

HOMES INSPIRED BY TRADITIONAL COUNTRY LIFE

FIFI O'NEILL

**FOREWORD BY CHRISTINA STRUTT,
CABBAGES & ROSES**

PHOTOGRAPHY BY MARK LOHMAN

CICO BOOKS
LONDON NEW YORK

This edition published in 2016 by CICO Books
An imprint of Ryland Peters & Small
20–21 Jockey's Fields   341 E 116th St
London WC1R 4BW   New York, NY 10029

www.rylandpeters.com

First published in 2011 by CICO Books

10 9 8 7 6 5 4 3 2 1

Text © Fifi O'Neill 2011
Design and photography © CICO Books 2011

A CIP catalog record for this book is available from the
Library of Congress and the British Library.

ISBN: 978 1 78249 328 0

Printed in China

EDITOR: Gillian Haslam   DESIGNER: Paul Tilby   PHOTOGRAPHER: Mark Lohman

To Louis, with love, always

Fifi

"Take this little thought from me,

You are what I want to be

All the kindly deeds you do,

Make me wish that I were you.

You are the finest of the fine,

Good, old loyal friend of mine."

CONTENTS

Foreword by Christina Strutt,
Cabbages & Roses 6

Introduction 8

FOREWORD
by Christina Strutt, Cabbages & Roses

This evocative tour of the cream of prairie homes, spanning thousands of miles, is testament to my friend Fifi O'Neill's unstoppable and inspiring energy and enthusiasm for all things beautiful. **Romantic Prairie Style** is a most charming record of houses and farmsteads dotted through the American homelands, reminding us of the history and endearing way of life, the traditions and spirit, barely changed since the houses were built.

Appearing almost untouched by brilliant twenty-first-century technological inventions—unimaginable when these houses were built—it is the enduring, wholesome creative charm that is worth photographing, writing about, and compiling into a book. This beautiful book on a beautiful subject, that can only have been put together by Fifi, with her outstanding ability to seek out the most compelling settings, will outlive the cleverest inventions and the newest technologies, and inspire many generations to come.

OPPOSITE and RIGHT Stone and wood outbuildings dot the prairie landscape and are prized for their organic and timeless beauty. Robust old pickup trucks are the ideal form of transportation and vintage ones are repainted in cheerful colors. Bales of hay, quilts, and animals herald the simpler life.

ABOVE Color and texture are the details that make this wholesome display oh-so prairie. The rugged, fading finish of the old pitcher balances the soft hues of hydrangeas to perfection. Vintage bottles and the sleek marble and weathered wood add contrast.

INTRODUCTION

THOUGH I WAS BORN IN THE CITY, I WAS ALWAYS A PRAIRIE GIRL AT HEART. I ALWAYS HAD A LOVE OF WIDE OPEN SPACES, WILD FLOWERS, AND UNCONTRIVED INTERIORS. Even as a child I was the happiest when the holidays came and my parents would take my sister and I away from Paris to a stone cottage in a meadow, deep in the heart of France. There life was pure, simple, and delightful. The landscape sparkled in unspoiled luminous clarity and it wasn't unusual to open the wooden shutters early in the morning and find a wayward cow or goat munching on dewy grass. Those were the days when we were free to jump feet first in limpid pools of rainwater, and gather armfuls of field flowers or baskets of fruits from adjacent orchards. On sunny afternoons the scent of freshly baked pies wafting from the kitchen would lure us back to the house.

Many years have passed. I moved far away and have lived in various countries, but these idyllic days and pastoral settings remained forever etched on my mind and influenced my decorating preferences wherever I called "home." The years I spent on the vast Manitoba and Illinois prairies only strengthened the primal feeling that comes from being in tune with the rhythms of nature and my affection for their ever-changing kaleidoscopic beauty grew even deeper.

Maybe it's a sign of the times, maybe it's the cyclical nature of life, but more than ever the world is longing to return to a simpler way of life. The upside of an unfavorable economy is that it makes us look inward, not just within ourselves but within our own settings. The benefits are measurable both emotionally and physically and clearly visible through the homes and lifestyles gracing the pages of this book.

I AM STANDING IN THE SUMMER SUN,

WHERE THE RABBITS HIDE AND THE SMALL QUAILS RUN.

I LISTEN TO THE PRAIRIE'S SONG

IN EVERY BREEZE THAT COMES ALONG.

BETTY LOU HEBERT, "PRAIRIE GENTIAN"

This is much more than a decorating book—it's is a way of life. One that reconnects us with what truly matters: family, home, and the earth. Honest materials, artisanal goods, and time-honored objects are once again valued and create homes, not just shelters. The lessons learned come together in the celebration of a wholesome life. Now, we look back to yesteryear because to understand the past is to secure the future. We embrace the present, hence fostering stewardship of the land. The authenticity and healing qualities inherent to this sustainable lifestyle define prairie style. Traditions and preservation are its heart. The nobility of the land and the fragility of our heritage are its soul. The spirit of prairie style drifts eternal in the romance of nurturing interiors and the abundant beauty of nature.

Fifi O'Neill

BELOW Romantic prairie is at its best when the rugged and the refined unite, as in this gentle mix of a pink alabaster lamp with a crackled nightstand wearing the patina of time.

BOTTOM Simple cotton and grain sac pillows look particularly inviting on a little wooden bench under dappled sunlight.

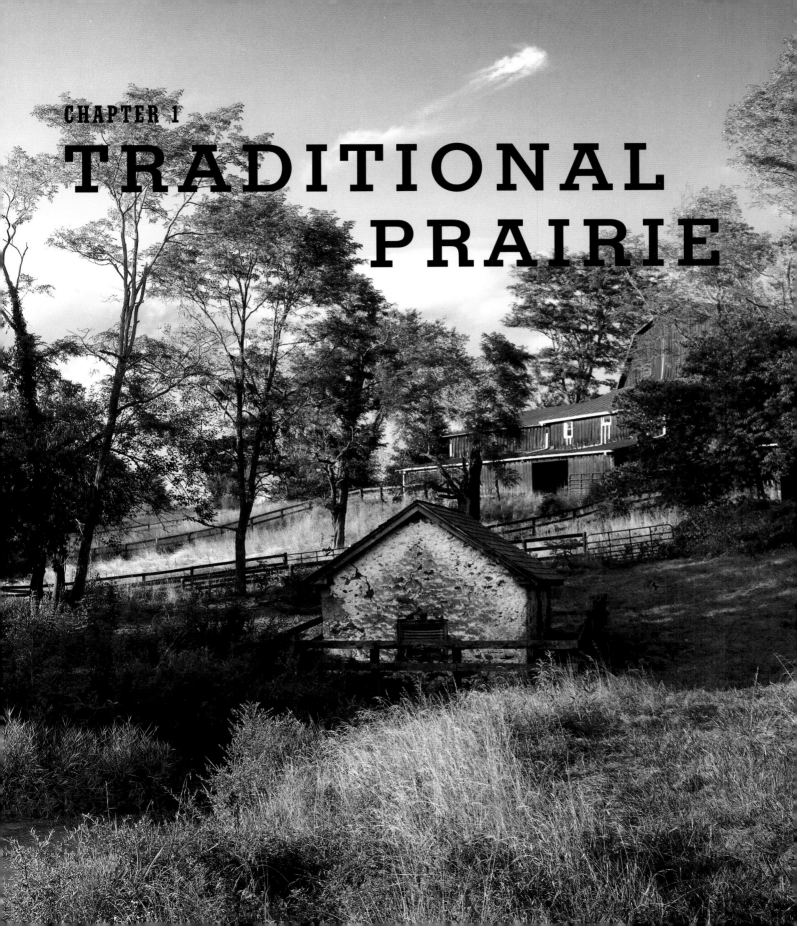

CHAPTER 1
TRADITIONAL PRAIRIE

LEFT AND RIGHT Set against a verdant cornfield backdrop, weathered outbuildings corral horses, Gilberta the goose, and Anne Marie's rare chickens. The original corn crib's ceiling makes a striking architectural statement. Jason added a ledge of old wood to a hand-carved mirrored shelf. A table dressed in vintage linens provides room for seasonal displays. Outdoor fun and indoor chores are an intrinsic part of farm life.

PIONEER SPIRIT

THE NARROW ROAD MEANDERS FOR MILES THROUGH LUSH CORN FIELDS AND PICTURESQUE PASTURES WHERE CATTLE AND HORSES GRAZE PEACEFULLY UNDER A CLOUDLESS SKY. One last bend of the twisting path reveals the entrance to Na-Da Farm and its four-square home. For Anne Marie, it was love at a first sight. The serene setting brought back memories of her childhood and spoke to her pioneer spirit. "I grew up on a farm in a small river town. There was an apple orchard in the back, a pond with a dock, a large barn, and a huge garden," she recalls. "My Hungarian great-grandmother used to sell the vegetables from her fields—which were plowed by a team

RILEY
FARM-RHYMES

LEFT AND ABOVE Family pieces
and repurposed finds set
against the wood's golden
caramel hue bring
character and warmth to
the living room. A favorite
book keeps company with
eggs from Gilberta, the
family's pet goose.

BELOW LEFT AND RIGHT Fabric remnants yield just enough material for drapes and cushions. A charming slipcover fashioned from a $3 sheet breathes life to an old armchair. Vintage and new pillows add comfort to a repainted bench. A former rabbit hutch stores linens and everyday items.

of horses steered by my grandfather—from the back of her pickup truck. One of my great-uncles, a horticulturist, grafted two plum trees to create the Gage plum. I cherish the values and lifestyle I was raised with, and my husband Jason and I are striving to instill these legacies in our five children."

One of the many features that compelled Anne Marie and Jason to purchase Na-Da farm was a unique old post-and-beam barn set right

OPPOSITE TOP AND BOTTOM Pillows hand sewn from old Scottish linens and French grain sacks cozy up the sleeping porch bed, while a garden gate is used to display sentimental items. Jason created the ceiling pattern from original bead board. Well-loved botanical books and sheet music are used daily.

in the center of the property. "It spoke of preservation and exuded potential to build future memories," Anne Marie remembers. "Jason and I worked side by side to create an area with reclaimed wood within the barn. At first it became the meeting place for my organic garden club, 'Na-Da Farm Chicks', then we added braces

LEFT A slender German carpenter's workbench, repurposed as a kitchen island, adds a handy work surface and doubles as a sideboard. The hutch provides storage while conveying old-world charm. Homemade preserves are made following family recipes. A resplendent sap bucket and a wire cup contribute homey and useful accents.

OPPOSITE An old orchard ladder ties in with the cabinets' window panes. Wire accessories give Anne Marie the flexibility to display favorite items. Upon removing the old linoleum, Jason unveiled the original Douglas fir flooring, which he meticulously refinished.

to the old hog panels to turn them into ample buffet tables for family gatherings, and furnished the barn with rescued and restored pieces from the 1940s." Their achievement was both a tribute to yesterday and an ode to tomorrow. The born-again barn soon became a haven for local artists and purveyors of vintage items to offer their art

and goods. "The interest for sharing our barn quickly grew and we decided to have our first barn sale," Anne Marie says. But, as fate would have it, a week before the event the barn went up in flames. What happened next epitomizes Anne Marie and Jason's indomitable pioneer spirit. "That Saturday night, our oldest son was to recite

a poem, 'The Charge of the Light Brigade' by Alfred Tennyson," Anne Marie says. "We watched him come on stage, armed with a sword, which was his great-grandfather's, unaware of the drama unfolding at the farm. By the time we got home the barn was in ruins and with it all the history, all the memories, all the plans." But this most unfortunate happening only helped Anne Marie and Jason to focus on what they still had—the farmhouse—and make the most of it. Jason, a carpenter by trade, built the living-room

ABOVE Hay topped with a hemp runner, a wing chair clad in a feminine slip, and a table dressed in diaphanous sheers symbolize the simple beauty of romantic prairie.

bookcases, installed the kitchen cabinets, refinished the floors, designed the new sunroom, and added the pergola-covered deck, while Anne Marie concentrated on repurposing accessories, decorating with antiques, collecting art, and hand sewing curtains, slipcovers, and clothes. "Linens and fabrics are what I have come to understand best through my own sewing. I have a deep appreciation for hand crochet and knitted items, and for the quality of old European textiles," she

SLOWLY, SILENTLY, NOW THE MOON

WALKS THE NIGHT IN HER SILVER SHOON

WALTER DE LA MARE

RIGHT Ringed by cornfields and framed by shade trees, a pair of Adirondack chairs provides a peaceful spot to rest from hours spent tending the potager.

ABOVE A weathered fence made from reclaimed corn crib siding adds authentic charm and structural definition to the potager, where Anne Marie applies the lessons learned from her great-grandmother to grow her vegetables for farm-to-table meals.

says. The charm of rooms furnished with affection, intimacy, and meaningful items, like family heirlooms and her collections of Native American artifacts, reflects Anne Marie's ability to carry on traditions and preserve the simpler way of life she loves. "Our home is all about easy, homemade comforts."

The connection between home and land is well-established, with the adjacent potager designed to supply not only vegetables but visual delight as well. "Designing our potager was one of the most rewarding things I have done on the farm," Anne Marie says. "We are a Certified Naturally Grown farm, which gives me the opportunity to farm just like my great-grandmother

ABOVE Anne Marie is very fond of outdoor living and sets little areas throughout the grounds where one can comfortably contemplate nature. A simple old iron bed heaped with a cushy duvet and pillows invites day dreams and reflection.

did. Being able to replicate her pioneer ways is very rewarding." Anne Marie revels in each of the prairie's seasons. Spring flies in on the wings of the songbird, vegetables from the potager herald summer, golden grass and milkweed's silken seeds signal fall. Even winter's ice storms provide beauty and enjoyment when the barn's foundation becomes a skating rink for the family. With every passing year, life on Na-Da farm comes full circle.

ABOVE Soft, faded floral and dainty pillows set against rugged and rusty iron and a perfectly weathered wall unite to create textural and visual appeal in a compelling tableau that unequivocally spells prairie charm, simple pleasures, and contentment.

OPPOSITE A vintage mirror juxtaposed with a pair of ceramic lambs unites elegant and rustic.

RIGHT Angela used a dry-brush technique to paint the crown molding to match the walls. A small cupboard, floor lamp, and settee in shades of blue are perfect companions. Flowers from the garden coordinate beautifully.

ELEGANT PRAIRIE

JUST OUTSIDE BUSTLING CHICAGO, THE ILLINOIS PRAIRIE STRETCHES LAZILY WITH HAY FIELDS DOTTED WITH CATTLE, OLD BARNS, HISTORICAL FARMHOUSES, AND SMALL PICTURESQUE TOWNS WITH QUAINT STREETS LINED WITH BRICK SHOPS THAT HARKEN BACK TO SIMPLER TIMES. And for Angela Reed, who, as she proudly states, comes "from a long line of farmwives and homemakers", the little town of McHenry compelled her and her husband Joel to move from a city townhouse back to the rural life of her youth.

A painted armoire fitted with chicken wire panels and a rugged harvest table balance the sophisticated crystal chandelier and the formal burled wood buffet. A grouping of vintage mirrors poised on the fireplace mantle, antique terra cotta planters, and a vibrant throw bring the gathered look that Angela favors.

The fact that every screen door of Angela's farmhouse slams every time they close is no accident. She wouldn't dream of fixing them. "I love the sound," she says. "It reminds me of the house in 'The Bridges of Madison County'— pale colored walls, big porcelain sink, and floral curtains."

Though her sense of home and her love of the American prairie are unquestionably deeply rooted in her early years, they share her heart with her passion for everything French,

Big copper pots imply large, heartwarming family gatherings and comfort food.

OPPOSITE Olive branches dancing along the walls, thyme drying on a peg, golden yarrow from the garden, a skirted sink, curtains in similar hues but with disparate patterns, and a fresh-from-the-oven herb quiche bring the colors and flavors of Provence to the kitchen.

particularly the farmhouses of Provence. By interspersing a few elegant pieces with homey rustic touches, Angela has created a look that says both farm and French. "We affectionately call our house the Parisienne Farmhouse and me, of course, Parisienne Farmgirl," she says.

Step into Angela's home and her infatuation with the warm colors of the south of France is cheerfully evident. From teal to periwinkle, shades of blue punctuated with spicy paprika and sunny yellows speak volumes. Add to that

ABOVE Angela's copper pots rank high on her list of favorite collections. "I love copper because it morphs," she says. "Whether wearing a brilliant glow, a subtly tarnished patina, or the timeless look of verdigris, it always speaks of a true working kitchen."

the salvaged furnishings she has painstakingly refurbished and you may as well be in the midst of the Midi, as the region is known to the French. From the dining room's sparkling chandeliers, tarnished mirrors, painted armoire, harvest table, and cushy armchairs to the kitchen's hand-painted tiles, glazed cabinets, and Venetian plaster walls, the rustic yet chic look mirrors the interior of a traditional Provençal mas (farmhouse). "Textures are important to me," Angela says. "Take Venetian plaster, for instance—it is a very elegant texture, almost cool to the touch like marble when finished properly. To keep it from being too shiny, I did not burnish it to a high gloss. It has just the right amount of depth and is much more interesting than plain paint and perfect for the feel I wanted for the kitchen." Because she strives to balance elegant and country, Angela explains, "If I do something daring and glamorous, like adding a satin pillow or a gilded chandelier, I offset it with something woven or tattered."

Equally handy with a needle, a saw, a paint brush, a shovel, a spade, or a spatula and a mixing bowl, whether she is making organic soaps, baking macaroons, reupholstering an old chair, designing her unique tiles, or tilling her garden, Angela is a homemaker par excellence. She is also a savvy shopper with an eye for pieces

ABOVE Angela is a consummate cook who loves to try recipes and experiment with new techniques. "I need a crisp, clean, bright, and cheery environment with everything right at my fingertips," she says. "I want the kitchen to look like a cook's kitchen. That's why I have hanging pots, stacks of pans of all sizes and shapes, and drying herbs. It's not a showroom. It's essentially a workroom."

ABOVE "Cabinets backed with painted and distressed bead board enhance the farmhouse feel," Angela explains. "Yellow and blue make such a happy color combination, and hand-painted tiles add another level of country charm."

with hidden potential, most of them acquired from barn sales, flea markets, and resale shops. "When you read about antiques, period furniture, textile houses, or regions of the world, you learn history and traditions," she says.

Angela wants her house to be livable yet lovely, "like the one I grew up in, full of delightful things—objects you can pick up and enjoy like old books or cushy pillows that the kids can use when making a fort, and where worn wood floors show signs of past use and welcome new scratches and nicks. If they were glossy and unscathed, it simply wouldn't work."

A sideboard made from
reclaimed wood keeps
cookbooks, iron stone,
and other useful items
on hand. Together with
a weathered post, it
tempers the elegance
implied by the chandelier.
The L-shaped counter
doubles as a convenient
prep area and place for
casual meals.

Angela is also partial to collections—from tarnished silver to shiny copper "for the sense of home they impart," she says. "Big copper pots imply large family gatherings and comfort food." But another important facet of her homesteading skills is firmly rooted in her farming background. That, and a gardening book on French kitchen gardens, inspired her to excavate a large part of her garden and build four wedge-shaped beds, now brimming with luscious vegetables, fragrant herbs, and edible flowers. "It's so comforting to

LEFT From sweet heirloom tomatoes, robust cabbage, and ambrosial herbs to edible blooms, the potager provides an abundance of produce for Angela to prepare flavorful and healthy meals for her family. Stone raised beds and gravel paths are as visually pleasing as they are useful. Little Amelie is already reaping the fruits of her mother's labor.

BELOW In keeping with all things homemade, a small branch is fashioned into a child-sized handrail.

walk out in the morning and pause under my apple trees, to feel the crunch of the gravel under my bare feet, pull a weed or pluck a strawberry, or harvest a tender lettuce and a plump tomato to go with just-baked bread. What could be more real?" Angela says. "My family, the house, the garden—that's what I know. That's what is real and the values I hold dear."

PRAIRIE SAVVY

WHEN JOY AND DON WALTMIRE'S HOME WAS BUILT, BACK IN THE 1800S, ITS STYLE WAS KNOWN AS A "POOR MAN'S VICTORIAN." NO FRILLS, NO GINGERBREAD—JUST A SIMPLE, BASIC FARMHOUSE, WHICH SUITED JOY JUST FINE. "I was charmed by the original wood floors, the nine-foot ceilings, the old millwork, and the potential for a wraparound porch," she says. But the rooms were in dire need of updating and it took foresight to envision the possibilities. Undaunted, Joy and Don primed, painted, polished, and preened, and reinvented their house into a home where simplicity meets substance.

OPPOSITE Curvaceous garden chairs sit invitingly against the charmingly weathered shed. A little bouquet nods to the garden nearby. Much-loved collections embrace the past.

RIGHT Life on the porch is all about comfort.

To balance the warm palette of the furnishings, Joy faux-finished the walls with a soft gray hue. With recycling and economy in mind, the sofa and ottoman are upholstered with fabric samples in similar hues with mixed patterns. Vintage gilded mirrors in varied sizes provide a focal point while maximizing the flow of natural light.

Joy's years spent attending auctions, estate sales, and flea markets began when she was just eight. "I would tag along with my dad to farms and learned about bidding," she recalls. "My mom loved antiques too and our home was furnished with pieces acquired at those sales." These early lessons were the foundation for her keen sense of values, her appreciation of vintage, and for developing her own trademark style. If one doubts the veracity of "one man's trash is another man's treasure", a look at Joy's savvy interior will quickly lay any suspicions to rest.

Throughout the farmhouse, layers of objects create layers of meanings that warm the heart and please the eye. From the artful way she displays her collections to the paint

ABOVE "The tarnish and the discoloring of old silver let each piece hold on to its uniqueness," Joy says. "I have always favored some imperfections."

THE WAY YOU PUT TOGETHER THE THINGS YOU LOVE COMES FROM THE WAY YOU FEEL ABOUT THEM.

The sign reads:

1 1/8 ACRES

MOUSTARDES:
HUILES de NOIX
GATEAUX aux NOIX
Coulis Framboises
Confitures
FRUITS au VIN
CROQUANTS aux NOIX
FOIS GRAS
TERRINES...

VINAIGRES:
VINS de Corse...

VERRERIES
SOUFFLEES

BREAD

ABOVE Though unexpected in a kitchen, a crackled mirror looks right at home. An old farm sign makes a perfect rustic companion for the wire bait bucket reborn as a lamp, while an aged board announcing kitchen staples adds a "farm fresh" flavor.

finishes she applied to walls and the manner in which she rethinks castoffs, Joy's touches imbue every room with a sense of history. "I discovered a farmers' market with antiques just a few blocks from the house and found many pieces to add to my collections of ironstone, zinc, wine baskets, brown transferware, and glass bottles," she says. "I am always on the hunt for items I can redo but sometime I keep in them in their original condition." Case in point is the sitting room's hand-hewn pine cubby. "It is old and rough in places but the patina was just right," Joy explains. "Though its intended use is not clear, it now serves as a showcase for collectibles and holds wine

bottles as if it had been made for them." Not much escapes Joy's inspired makeovers. A cement bust's mottled patina sparked the idea for the walls' gray wash. "I mixed, poured, and tested until I achieved the look of old cement," she says. "I applied the mixture with a brush, then wiped off the excess with a damp cloth in a sweeping motion to get just the right texture." When in need of additional storage, she swiftly skirted a console with a striped fabric that provided the solution with an off-the-shoulder insouciance.

At the time Don and Joy first moved in, the kitchen reflected the home's humble beginnings. But rather than invest in costly improvements, Joy

ABOVE The vintage post was added to complement the original scalloped wood valence. A table top resting over a storage cabinet offers a cozy spot for relaxed meals. The realistic but faux fieldstone backsplash is nothing more than an inexpensive wallpaper border.

ALL OBJECTS TELL A STORY AND HAVE AN ORIGINAL PURPOSE, BUT THEIR FORMER USE SHOULD NOT NEGATE A NEW FUNCTION.

OPPOSITE A burlap moving pad and a linen skirt conceal a makeshift desk. The little crystal chandelier injects a feminine note in the rustic study.

ABOVE Old lamp bases were rethought into elegant candlesticks. A favorite thrift shop coverlet and floral pillows temper the bedroom's moody palette. The table—a curbside find —was stripped, sanded, and buffed to reveal its rugged beauty.

heeded her favorite mantra: work with what you have! "I imagined a different kind of farmhouse flair, a marriage of vintage and industrial," she says. "Every day I would look at the potting shed's rusty tin roof and it gave me the idea for developing a faux finish that mimics old tin. I experimented with several colors until I found the formula that most resembles that oxidized look and came up with the patina for the cupboards."

Her resourcefulness results in unique decorating ideas: old bait wire buckets become light fixtures, a tin fragment salvaged from her

grandfather's chicken coop makes a little awning, a primitive pulley holds a crystal chandelier. Her affection and respect for items of the past go further than refurbishing and repurposing once-loved but discarded or damaged pieces. Old farm ledger records, vintage posters, and faded photographs and postcards have become a source for a line of artwork named "grittyandgreen" that illustrates her love of family and traditions. By fusing vintage documents and photos to parchment paper, Joy creates one-of-a-kind images overlaid on wood. A very special one, made with a picture of her dad standing by his old pickup truck, takes pride of place in the sitting room. "All items tell a story and have an original purpose," Joy says. "But a former use should not negate a new function. The way you put together the things you love comes from the way you feel about them."

Evocative wicker sports a
black finish and toile and
striped pillows reminiscent
of softly faded denim.
Zinc crates add simple
decorative accents.

OPPOSITE Architectural
remnants give extra charm
to the shed, while a rustic
hutch stores gardening
essentials and doubles as
a potting bench.

Carol Spinski's Missouri home is a love letter to her mom and her favorite prairie style. "As a little girl growing up in Arkansas, I watched my mother, Stella Mae, treat laundry days not as a chore but as a rite of comfort," she reminisces. "Being a true farm girl, my mom would always soak her linens in a mixture of buttermilk, water, and lemon juice to make sure the cotton remained pristine."

REFINED PRAIRIE

As the years went by, that lovely memory, together with many more from her young days, set the course for Carol's pursuit of that simpler lifestyle. "I long dreamed of a farmhouse of my own and when I found it I knew it was the perfect one," she

LEFT Collections are grouped by color and theme. Whether set in a mason jar on a chair or propped in a zinc bucket next to Jadeite, contrasting colors and textures prevail. The porch welcomes with homey accoutrements. The foyer's crisp purity reveals the home's aesthetics.

RIGHT Blooms in watering cans and buckets bring home the lush prairie.

says. "It had been built in 1865 by a farmer for his wife and nine children and had all the right features, including two front porches, gingerbread trim, stained glass doors, high ceilings, crown molding, and cozy window seats."

To make the most of the historic architectural features and set a quiet backdrop for furnishings slip-covered in linen and faded textiles, Carol chose a fresh and serene whisper-soft palette of cream, vanilla, and gray, and dressed the windows in barely-there light-filtering cheesecloth. "Keeping the pale hues flowing from one room to the next was the best design decision I made," she says. "It allowed me to use all the vintage

ABOVE AND OPPOSITE Next to a French buffet wearing its original paint, a birdcage sits on an old fishing basket. A diminutive stool acts as a pedestal for delicate blooms. The height of French doors and salvaged columns lends balance to the stately armoire. The chandelier adds an air of romantic elegance.

In keeping with true prairie-style kitchens, open shelving and free-standing hutches take preference over fixed cupboards and offer movable flexibility. Natural stone, mixed metals, and pine flooring provide a neutral yet textural background. The bakery sign and the leaded glass door act as vintage art. A sunny window sill keeps potted herbs on hand.

pieces I saved over the years." Like an artist painting on a blank canvas, she selected from her collection of salvaged and family antiques to bring a feeling of quiet beauty to each space. "My mom taught me to appreciate found pieces with wonderful patina and original paint," she says. Though uncluttered, the rooms do not feel cold or sparse as their simplicity is balanced by the warm of honey-hued pine floor, the appeal of imperfections inherent in natural fabrics such as cotton and raw linen, and a pleasing medley of handmade baskets, pottery, and blown glass

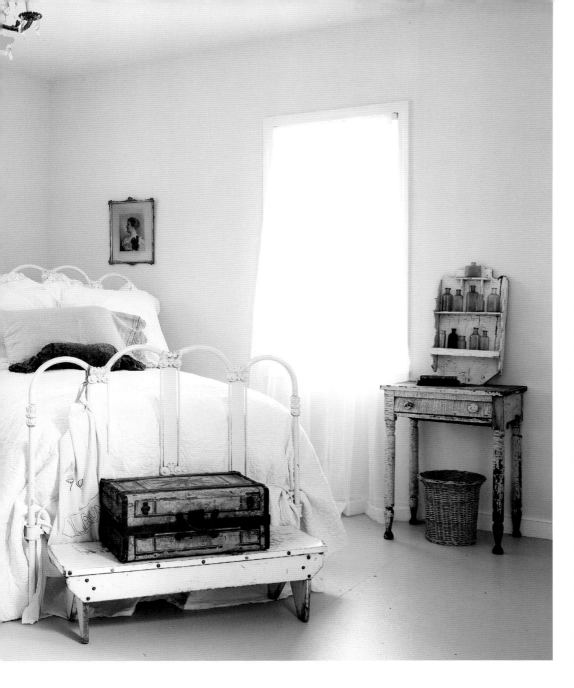

OPPOSITE ᴀɴᴅ LEFT Her daughter's childhood bed was Carol's inspiration for the romantic bedroom. Accessories in faded hues heighten the comfort quotient of the pale palette. A collection of milk glass coordinates with the gently worn dresser, while a monogrammed towel attached with wooden clothespins to gossamer curtains pays tribute to Carol's mother. An unassuming garden bench and chair contribute to the room's soothing freshness.

bottles selected for their timeless appeal. "Homespun and artisanal elements not only keep the pale color palette from getting boring by adding interest, but they are also favored staples of this significant style, because they tell a tale of yesteryear," Carol says.

But while paying tribute to the home's history was a must, incorporating a touch of glamour and an occasional modern vibe play a part in preventing the interior from looking dated and demonstrate that opposites do, indeed, attract. Antique crystal chandeliers—some large, others

discreet—cast a romantic glow in every room, including the kitchen where a sparkling one, centered above the island (made from a standard cabinet paired with sculptural corbels and a tumbled marble top) shares the limelight with contemporary pendants set over the original porcelain sink and the new countertops. In the dining room, the juxtaposition of then and now is epitomized by the union of the table's newly minted iron legs and a reclaimed wood top and vintage chairs.

Whether sipping sweet tea on the porch swing on a warm summer afternoon, celebrating festive occasions with family and friends in the dining room, or gathered for a picnic under the big oak tree in the backyard, the farmhouse answers Carol's dream and echoes her childhood memories. Following in her mother's footsteps, she now enjoys her own laundry days, complete with her homemade recipe for keeping pristine linens. The tradition lives on.

My mother, Stella Mae, treated laundry days not as a chore but as a rite of comfort.

LEFT Freshly laundered linens on a line perpetuate a cherished family ritual.

BELOW Wire and wood accessories are visually pleasing and practical.

OPPOSITE A prettily sun-faded tablecloth, rustic seating, and a farmhouse table laden with tempting treats set the stage for quintessential and charming prairie fare.

PERFECT PRAIRIE

IN THEIR QUEST FOR THE QUIET PLEASURES OF
COUNTRY LIFE, ANTIQUE DEALERS CAROLINE
VERSCHOOR AND HER HUSBAND JON PAUL SAUNIER
FOUND EVERYTHING THEY HOPED FOR, AND MUCH
MORE: "WE WANTED AN OLD HOUSE, WITH SOME
LAND AND PREFERABLY A WORKING BARN THAT WE
COULD USE TO STORE OUR SHIPMENTS OF FURNITURE
FROM EUROPE," CAROLINE SAYS. "We had been
looking for years when a friend urged me to take
a look at a property—a prosperous dairy farm
back in the 1800s—near Hamilton, Virginia. Not
only was the farmhouse a perfect Colonial with
a symmetrical center-hall and four nicely sized
rooms on each floor, but it also came with a huge
barn, a spring house, a corn crib, a little pond,

LEFT The deck is a favorite
spot for convivial gatherings
and offers front-row seats
to witness amethyst skies and
magnificent sunsets. A
venerable oak tree and open
fields conspire to give the
house a picture-perfect
setting. Daughter Gwenael
shares playtimes with
friend Alice. Roscoe, the
family mutt, stands guard.

RIGHT Gweneal and sister
Sophie gather field flowers.

Wool throws. raw linen, and a woven rug bring cozy, tactile accents to the sofa and chair, while the aged coffee table and Swedish clock provide a vintage vibe. For impact as well as simplicity, the abacus is the only wall art.

and ten acres of the most stunning rolling hills." Though Caroline did not study interior design, it has always been a passion of hers. "I read a lot of books and magazines on the subject and ten years ago I took a leap of faith and opened a shop," she says. "But we closed it when we moved here because the barn is the idyllic location for that purpose." In decorating her home Caroline aimed for an interior that would suit the needs of a modern family as well as satisfy her and Jon Paul's affinity for simple beauty. She successfully met their goal with rooms that marry the streamlined aesthetic of Scandinavian farmhouse design with the sink-in and laid-back comfort that are staples of the American prairies. "I selected a chalky palette color for most of the rooms, except for the

ABOVE In the summer, the fireplace remains a focal point stacked with naturally bleached wood that adds presence to the hearth. Stained to a rich brown, ancient French shutters conceal a storage closet.

RIGHT The buffet's layers of paint were stripped to reveal the wood's original grain. A woven trunk presents an attractive alternative to a coffee table. Vintage chairs are elegantly clad in prized French fabric.

UNDERSTATED TRANQUIL SPACES ARE WARMED BY THE TONAL VARIETY AND TEXTURES OF MANY BELOVED OBJECTS.

ABOVE The library desk, a former table with a marble slab set atop an iron base, juxtaposes pleasingly with one of Caroline's restored armchairs. Jon Paul built the shelves and added a barn door sliding rail, to which he attached the old apple ladder.

bathrooms and the kitchen where I opted for a more grayish shade of white," Caroline explains. "These hues have always worked for me and I think they give the farmhouse that cozy, old-world feel compared to white, which would have made it more modern than it really is." The understated tranquil spaces are warmed by the tonal variety and textures of many

RIGHT The family-style kitchen was created by joining two rooms together. The island, an old oak store counter from Belgium, provides a subtle separation as well as a connection for both spaces.

OPPOSITE TOP A versatile old hospital stainless-steel cart is used as an extra set of shelves to display silver, glassware, and linens and acts as a small buffet or bar for parties on the deck.

OPPOSITE BOTTOM Black granite proves a good foil for a white farmhouse sink and stainless-steel appliances. "We chose frosted glass cabinetry to create a more transparent feel while avoiding staring at every spice jar," Caroline says.

beloved objects. "I like to accessorize with lots of antique finds, old books, boxes, and other trinkets that are typically of little financial value but hold deep emotional meaning for me," she says. "I am also a big fan of natural treasures such as shells and antlers, and rocks and corals."

Caroline is also partial to the right mix of "new antiques" and true antiques, something she was exposed to while growing up in the Netherlands. "When you have too many true antiques, the look can become heavy and oppressive and too many Modernistic pieces

run the risk of creating a sterile and cold environment," she notes. Whether she gathers goods from her regular trips to her native country or from local auctions, Caroline's mission is to reclaim the beauty of old pieces and give them a new life. And under her touch, remnants of the past are made whole again. Long before it became fashionable, she was incorporating vintage textiles in her original designs and the fabrics with which she reupholsters old armchairs have become one of her trademarks. "Their timeworn frames have a distinctively beautiful

mellow patina but, as a rule, their original coverings are much tattered. Ten years ago, I came up with the idea of revamping them with old grain sacks from Europe and now I am also using vintage paisleys and fabrics from India," she says. Her modern sensibilities coupled with her reinterpretation of classic furnishings blend into a unique personal style, where new and old pieces play off each other harmoniously with a relaxed, put-up-your-feet sophistication.

ABOVE Designed to promote a peaceful environment, the bedroom, though sparsely furnished, invites with a canopied bed with lightweight linens and panels reminiscent of a cocoon.

The simplicity of each room allows each piece to stand out and sends a message that whispers rather than shouts Caroline's connection to her roots and her respect for her heritage; it also demonstrates her ability to bring new life to classic designs. Refurbishing pieces herself, recycling (whether by gathering natural elements or purchasing items made with pre-used materials, like the collection of pink-hued glass candlesticks on the living-

BELOW A linen-clad bench adds a comfortable place to sit near the tub. Bath essentials are kept handy in an heirloom cask atop a primitive stool.

A CHALKY PALETTE GIVES THE FARMHOUSE THAT COZY, OLD-WORLD FEEL COMPARED TO WHITE, WHICH WOULD HAVE MADE IT MORE MODERN THAN IT REALLY IS.

LEFT AND ABOVE A old farmhouse cabinet and a long meat hook from Belgium serve a useful purpose for storing riding and winter gear. A weathered bench and wild flowers left to dry in baskets and a canvas bag add to the rustic room's pastoral simplicity.

OPPOSITE Like a lacy veil, the delicate cow parsley covers the prairie with a multitude of intricate white blossoms. Sophie and Gwenael share summer days helping in the barn and searching for bullfrogs in the the mirror-like pond.

room buffet) or repurposing stately French shutters into closet doors and acquiring windows and inexpensive tiles for the mud room, Caroline always has preservation and budget in mind.

Expressive original art, like the family room abacus—the work of artist Greg Hannan—also plays a role in the evocative decorating scheme. "His work tells a story and beautifully ties with my love for found objects and neutrality," Caroline explains. Vintage signs are equally embraced. A handsome one, originally from an old inn, makes a strategic focal point in the kitchen, while the living room displays a graphic farm sale board which, by coincidence, features Caroline's name.

"Life is about respecting the past and embracing the present and the changes that come with it," Caroline says. "This is our updated version of Little House on the Prairie. We love the wholesome life we are giving our children. Home is where the heart is."

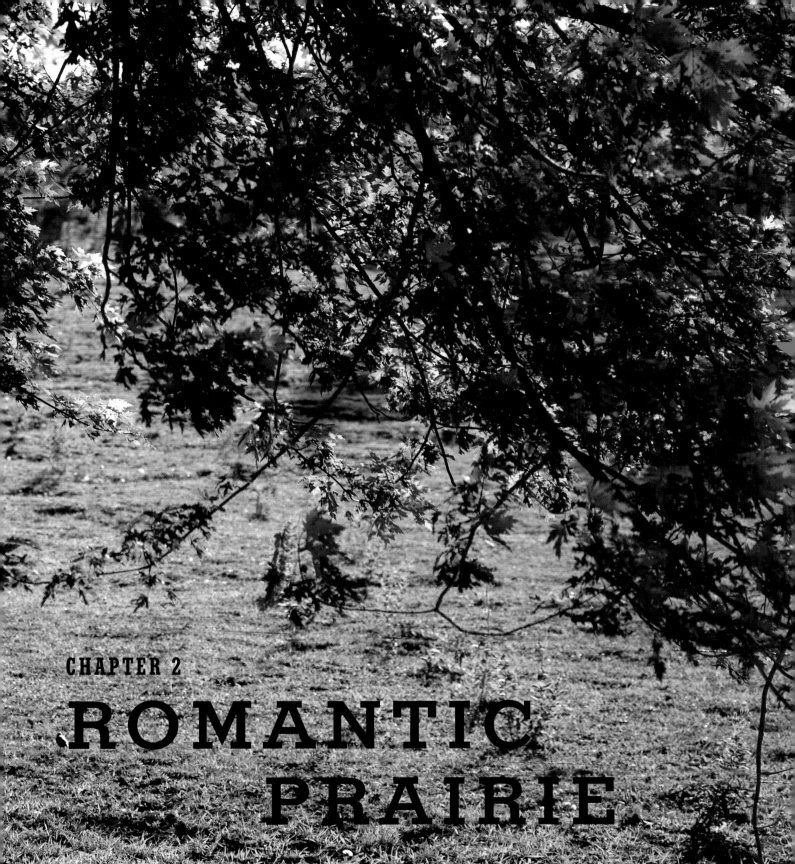

CHAPTER 2
ROMANTIC
PRAIRIE

OPPOSITE Dark floors make a warm foil for a pastel palette and weathered furniture, while blush-pink hydrangeas add a lively dash of color. Eiderdowns in faded paisleys call attention to timeless comfort. Flowers and greenery are soft counterparts to textured garden urns. Dressed with a floral sheet and a fluffy duvet, a plain umbrella and cot become a garden hideaway.

RIGHT AND BELOW From the antique doorstop to the bed linens and chair, gentle colors define the little house.

PRAIRIE INFLUENCES

CHRISTIAN MCCORD AND HER HUSBAND BRYAN DON'T LIVE IN A FARMHOUSE OR A CABIN IN A MEADOW, BUT IN A QUAINT COTTAGE IN A CALIFORNIA BEACH TOWN. Yet their home is a perfect example of the adaptability and versatility of prairie style's endearing charm. Christian grew up in bucolic Virginia and knows the advantages of a simpler lifestyle. Though miles away from the rolling hills of her childhood, the quiet and picturesque setting of the small 1925 home was equally appealing to her for settling down and raising Lily and Noah, the couple's two young children.

Under Christian's touch, the once neglected little house blossomed into a sumptuously cozy and beautifully rustic haven. Her choice of a soft, almost fragile, palette stems from the sea-glass, sun-bleached hues and wave-washed shells of the nearby beach.

The cozy, light-filled living room owes its quietly romantic feel to the contrasting simplicity of soft and rugged furnishings. The oversized couch, heaped with a feather duvet and pillows, extends a pampering invitation while the informality of the garden chair and bench capture the simple contentment that exemplifies prairie style. Christian's affinity for faded florals was the trigger for her collection of prettily painted old doorstops.

LEFT Flirty curtains and floral cushions with a sun-faded motif have a feminine allure. Chipped folding chairs, wicker, and sideboards play down the elegance of the chandelier.

RIGHT AND ABOVE Disparate objects are united in an exquisitely textural composition. In the dining room, cast-iron accessories, architectural salvage, and a battered hutch underscore Christian's affinity for authentic vintage and prairie style.

Armoires, tables, benches, and chairs wear similarly tender finishes that sooth their rugged style. "They have a history. They have been loved and stood the test of time," Christian says. "They comfort me." Her respect for their past life is visible in the way she doesn't attempt to alter their original paint or patina. "I only buy what is authentically vintage and something that I am absolutely in love with," she says.

There is a deliberately unstudied appeal to Christian's decorating approach that gives the rooms a casual feel of beauty and function.

FAR LEFT TOP The pink perfection and sprig pattern of this gently rumpled apron bring to mind the easy grace of days gone by and time spent gathering herbs from the garden to prepare flavorful meals.

FAR LEFT BOTTOM Accessorizing with outdoor items is one of Christian's decorating trademarks. Parading atop a vintage hutch, galvanized watering cans nod to the nearby garden.

LEFT TOP Iconic enamel has long been a staple of country kitchens and prairie life. This beautiful blue bowl's chipped coating tells of years of usefulness.

LEFT BOTTOM Unfitted open shelves stacked with simple, durable dinnerware foster a relaxed, inviting feel.

Oversized and overstuffed couches, stacks of snugly eiderdowns, and piles of cushy pillows denote a predominance for comfort. Intended for the outdoors, chairs, benches, and concrete urns and statuary bring the garden within. Rooms flow from one to the next as pastel hues and aged furnishing create a unified visual. Whether chosen for their textures, colors, or meanings, accessories—from a dainty cup to a fabric-covered photo album and a collection of doorstops—are as much part of the main scheme as the furniture. Hardwood floors stained a rich chocolate brown add dimension to the small rooms and highlight rather than obscure the

RIGHT An old French wire stand filled with colorful fruit imparts a fresh country atmosphere. A tall, narrow English cabinet dating back to the 1890s is repurposed as an island in the newly remodeled galley-style kitchen. The rose painting and chandelier add a whimsically romantic flourish. Christian kept the pantry door in its natural state to tie in with the new butcher-block counter and contribute an added element of texture. Shelves provide storage while maintaining a sense of openness that a traditional cupboard could not offer. Daisies, lisianthus, and lavender are evocative of a cutting garden.

HAVE NOTHING IN YOUR HOUSE THAT YOU DO NOT KNOW TO BE USEFUL, OR BELIEVE TO BE BEAUTIFUL.

WILLIAM MORRIS

overall palette by providing a warm contrast.

While each room was given a cosmetic makeover, the kitchen underwent a more substantial facelift. "Even though I loved the original cabinets, they couldn't be salvaged," Christian says. "But I still wanted the room to have a vintage character and also be fully

functional and have an open feel." New white
bead-board cabinets, open shelves strategically
positioned near a window, and an old hutch
and weathered island deliver the right mix of
elements and accents.

Christian uses every inch of her compact
cottage, but in a way that never feels overdone
or cramped. In spite of its location, the McCords'
home is a tribute to the iconic prairie traits of
comfort and ease, and quiet romance.

Though equal in simplicity and comfort, Lily's and Noah's bedrooms are distinguished from one another by their color and furnishings. The faded hues of a favorite paisley eiderdown (below) inspired Christian to wrap the bedroom in a mellow palette of subtle yellow, aqua, cream, and green.

LEFT AND OPPOSITE The old
pickup truck, chickens
roaming freely, and aprons
hung to dry paint a charming
tableau of prairie life.
Accessories in muted shades
contribute to the foyer's
inviting feel. Tied together,
the ragged pages from an
old book act as a piece of
art. Touches of green
enliven the purity of a white
vignette. A floral quilt
provides a cozy spot for
picnics in the meadow.

FOR SOME PEOPLE, FINDING THEIR DREAM PRAIRIE HOME WITHIN
THE SETTING THEY SEEK OFTEN TAKES A LONG TIME. BUT NOT SO
FOR ANDREA AND EUGENE DICKERSON.

NOSTALGIC PRAIRIE

Once they made up their mind to move from California to
Nebraska, fate lend a helping hand in the unlikely form of
an internet advertisement offering a circa-1890 farmhouse.
They faxed the owner an offer and the next day the house
was theirs. They soon packed their two young sons, Justin
and Ethan, and their belongings and, like the pioneers of
yore, traveled to the heartland to live their dream. As they
approached their destination, they followed a country road

The window seat and
bookshelves are new
additions to the dining
room. The shelves provide
room for Andrea to neatly
display collections of
ironstone, baskets, silver,
old wooden boxes, buckets,
dinnerware, and spools
of twine to bring tactile
elements that warm the
understated yet welcoming
room. Pillows dressed in
vintage fabric cozy up the
the window bench. Poised
on a cane chair, a sweet
floral cushion imparts
a touch of femininity.

ABOVE A sleek ironstone bowl
cradling spools of twine;
cream pitchers with a smooth
finish paired with books
with brownish hues and
worn covers; the intricate
patterns of silverware atop
lustrous dishes—all create
the intentional contrast of
surfaces and textures that
Andrea favors to impart
depth and dimension to the
neutrality of her palette.

LEFT AND OPPOSITE Just-laid eggs from the hens and fresh flowers from the fields are farmhouse favorite staples. Handmade barn lights recall traditions, while an old dresser with a new bead-board back and towel bar attests to Andrea's creative repurposing.

rambling through rolling hills and fields of corn and alfalfa grown in perfect rows. "The first time we saw our new home, and the town of Blair, was when we pulled up with our moving truck," Andrea says. "It was exactly what we thought it would be. The house was charming, the setting picture perfect, and the little town very quaint."

They settled and Andrea began to make the old farmhouse hers. "I wanted a calm and simple place," she says. A palette of paints with evocative names like "snowfall white", "gray owl", and "seashell" accomplished the desired effect. Furniture showing signs of age and imperfections enhances the sense

THE FAIREST HOME I EVER KNEW

WAS FOUNDED IN AN HOUR

BY PARTIES ALSO THAT I KNEW

A SPIDER AND A FLOWER —

A MANSE OF MECHLIN AND OF FLOES

EMILY DICKINSON

LEFT AND RIGHT The bedroom mixes touches of rustic and refinement with cool blue accents for a simply serene setting. Mirrors of different sizes and shapes maintain the uncluttered look that Andrea prefers, yet add a subtle decorating hint. The floor is kept bare to allow its rich hue and grain to play a part in the decor. Antlers, old books, and raw wood are all about tone and texture.

of permanence and comfort. "This is one instance where color doesn't matter because a quick coat or two of paint will make any piece fit in," Andrea says. "Older pieces have a nostalgia no new piece could ever have. I love to know that by giving them a new purpose I am contributing to their survival." To maintain the serene mood, Andrea controls clutter with accessories kept in the same color family but with varied textures that allow them to stand on their own.

Her new lifestyle has awakened a new interest and a new skill. She has taught herself to sew and made slipcovers and chair pads, and little pillows in her favorite fabrics. "Self-sufficiency is a good skill to have when you live on the prairie," she

says. That is also why, soon after moving, she and Eugene acquired three goats, two geese, several hens and a rooster, and "Stella", a 1949 Ford pickup truck for running local errands or bringing home bags of chicken and goat feed and bales of hay. Andrea says, "We found what we wished for—a simpler and happier, more fulfilling life."

ABOVE A gentle breeze wafts the scents of the prairie through the drying laundry.

TOP LEFT Nico the goat is free to roam about, as are all the other family pets.

BOTTOM LEFT A painted bucket pairs up with vibrant blooms in a fetching vignette

OPPOSITE, ABOVE A makeshift potting bench and a seasoned chair are the perfect garden companions.

OPPOSITE, BOTTOM A refurbished $6 thrift-store sofa and a weathered bench invite relaxation on the sheltered front porch.

OPPOSITE A soft palette allows for easy detail changes without needing to repaint rooms. Keeping the color scheme within the same family provides continuity from one room to the next. An old orchard ladder and an unpainted side table add definition and texture with a country flair that balances the more formal style of the dining-room table and fireplace.

RIGHT Old doors help to define areas and impart a sense of age to the new home.

TRACEY LEBER IS NOT NEW TO THE ILLINOIS PRAIRIE LIFE. SHE GREW UP ONLY TWENTY MINUTES FROM THE HOME SHE SHARES WITH HER HUSBAND STEVE AND THEIR THREE CHILDREN.

PRAIRIE PRETTY

"After college I spent a few years in Chicago, but when we decided to start a family we wanted our children to grow up in the quiet beauty of the area that brought me so much happiness as a child," Tracey says. Moving from a small 1915 bungalow to a newly built and more spacious home also seemed like a good idea, since it would allow her to spend

TOP RIGHT A sideboard, kept in its original condition, is paired with an architectural window to add depth and dimension to the pastel palette. The spacious buffet plays double duty for storage and as a serving area.

BOTTOM RIGHT A tall vintage hutch with glass panes allows favorite and everyday items like dishes and flatware to become part of the decor. The zinc bucket holds a simple bunch of flowers gathered from a nearby field.

FAR RIGHT Passed on from one generation to the next, the dining-room set exemplifies the value of inherited pieces dear to prairie style. "It was in my grandparents' home for 65 years," Tracey says. "When I think of all of the family gatherings that centered around that table and my grandmother serving her home-cooked meals there, it brings back fond memories." Aqua seltzer bottles and mason jars contribute to the nostalgic, heartfelt setting.

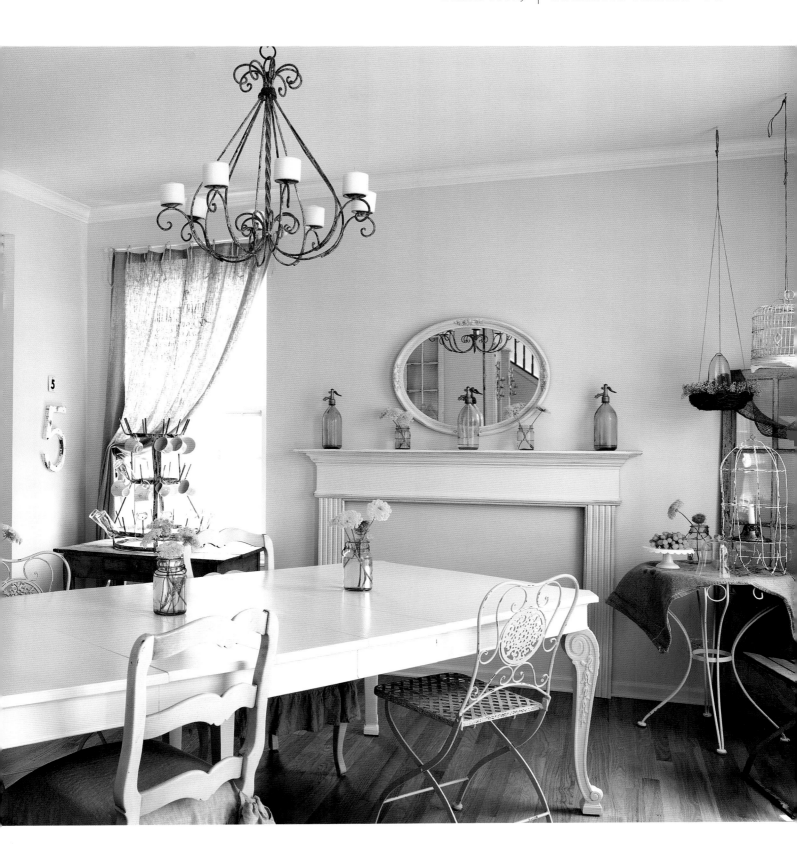

ABOVE Pages from a favorite book held with vintage seam binding to the frames of old English windows create a unique display. A painted desk and chair add to the charming yet practical space.

time with her small children rather than having to attend to their former home's constant need for repairs. But soon after making the move, she realized she was missing the character her old house had. To remedy the situation she began filling the rooms with architectural salvage and vintage pieces. Hardwood floors were also high on Tracey's wish list. "They instantly add character, recall those of farmhouses, and work

ABOVE Once used to corral small tools, a perfectly tattered metal box finds a new purpose as the keeper of favorite jewelry. Its top provides a shelf for fresh and dry bouquets.

ABOVE A subdued blue-and-white scheme underscores this cozy bedroom's gentle mix of textures. Plump pillows fashioned from sun-faded blue and gray mattress ticking create a pleasing contrast to the white bedding.

well with vintage pieces," she says. "A comfortable and inviting home with a sense of family and history has always been important to me." Though she admits not being an expert with regard to antiques, she does have a definite grasp of the worth of older pieces, especially those with sentimental value. "Many of our furnishings are inherited," she says. "Well-used and much-loved family heirlooms instantly bond us to our home. Pieces that I truly love, not pieces that are 'in' or trendy, also contribute a timeless mood."

From soft green to pale blue, the rooms share a common pale palette with furniture painted in various shades of whites. "I have been very

influenced by the decorating style of the Scandinavian countries, especially where they have worked French pieces into their designs," Tracey explains. "I love the way they use painted furniture, slipcovers, and vintage accessories to create a beautiful, calm, serene flow to their homes. I have always been attracted to white, but I never buy the same shade of white paint twice, which produces more warmth and coziness."

In fact, Tracey is always repainting something. "You have to pick pieces based on their shape or

WELL-USED AND MUCH-LOVED FAMILY HEIRLOOMS INSTANTLY BOND US TO OUR HOME.

OPPOSITE, TOP "Every room should have at least one metal element to help ground the space," Tracey says. "When the pieces also have history, like the French bistro chair, I love them even more because I imagine where they might have been before."

OPPOSITE, BOTTOM The day bed and old barn doors express Tracey's love of Nordic style.

BELOW Gauzy panels and simple, graphic garden chairs show the beauty of contrasting textures and how the right placement of outdoor furniture can work indoors.

detailing, not just their color. Anything can be transformed with paint."

Tracey is often tweaking her surroundings to keep them fresh. Flea markets and thrift shops are her favorite source for affordable finds. "I swap out some of the smaller details as my tastes change, but always keep the main pieces the same. Therefore, that sense of connection to our home and family remains deeply rooted and constant."

OPPOSITE The very elements that define romantic prairie style come together in the unstudied simplicity of this organic display.

RIGHT Weathered, handmade, heartfelt, and homespun are at the root of textural appeal.

BELOW A touch of lace and a fabric flower take a straw hat from plain to fanciful.

MY MODEST 1920S VERNACULAR COTTAGE CAME WITH AN OPEN FIELD AND A DILAPIDATED OUTBUILDING. AS STRANGE AS IT MAY SEEM, THE LATTER WAS ONE THE REASONS I BOUGHT THE PROPERTY.

PRAIRIE CHIC

Its sun-bleached tin roof, open rafters, and raw wood walls had the seductive appeal of the old barns that grace the Canadian prairie where I lived for many years, and where the seed of my love affair with this style was sown. The rundown shed, as everyone used to call it, remained in that derelict state until I could finally dedicate time to the improvements that would take it from dreary to dreamy. Today, walls rebuilt from reclaimed

wood stand firmly on a reinforced concrete foundation, a new tin roof keeps the monsoon rains out where they belong, and salvaged windows allow the natural light in.

I have always been compulsive regarding old furniture. Over the years I have amassed more than I need and the barn, as I call it, offered an instant answer for my excesses and a no-cost decorating solution.

There are many variations on the prairie-style theme, but all share common characteristics, among them a love and respect for traditions and honest materials, a need for tranquility and simplicity, and a spontaneity of design, be it rustic, refined, or understated chic.

Prairie-style decorating doesn't answer to a set of rules but responds

LEFT AND OPPOSITE Items with contrasting finishes and shapes are both romantic and organic. The faux fireplace comes alive with the glow of a candle. Hand-cut glass tiles and a Venetian mirror nod to elegance.

The dove gray and chalky white palette allows furnishings to reveal their simple lines. The loose-weaved burlap curtains filter the bright sunlight with a shadowy softness. Robust zinc, wrought iron, and wood objects juxtaposed with fragile glass and soft-hued accessories define the refined rusticity of the barn and enhance its understated chic.

A vintage fabric remnant and burlap panels keep a small refrigerator and storage out of sight. Though sparsely furnished, the little kitchen offers all necessary amenities. The weathered table is the right size and the perfect color.

to a personal sense of comfort and beauty. For me, that spells freedom and creativity. My own taste leans toward a refined rusticity, a look easily accomplished with pre-loved pieces, whisper-soft colors, romantic accents, eloquent objects, and a do-it-yourself attitude. For example, the faux plank floor is the result of necessity. Though I would have loved to use the real thing, the cost was prohibitive. Instead, gnarly, rough plywood, once painted and white

washed, provided a similar result at a fraction of the price. A working fireplace was also a tempting addition but a major expense, and, considering the balmy Florida

ABOVE Uncontrived arrangements perpetuate the clutter-free, subdued theme. A tiny chandelier and a mirror send a discreetly elegant note.

**HOME, THE SPOT OF EARTH SUPREMELY BLEST,
A DEARER, SWEETER SPOT THAN ALL THE REST.**

ROBERT MONTGOMERY

winters, an unwarranted one. An old mantel set a few inches away from the wall and filled with branches proved a pleasing compromise. Inexpensive burlap may not have the pedigree of antique linen, but trimmed with lace remnants from an old nightgown, it sends a vintage message in the same way an organza blouse elevates a faded pair of jeans.

BELOW AND OPPOSITE The area where the roof slopes down lends itself to a sleeping nook overlooking the garden. Pillows handmade from vintage fabrics endow the simple bed with charm and comfort. The quaint, whitewashed shutters were recycled from the upper panels of an old armoire, and, together with the scalloped metal bedside table and the curvy iron chandelier—spray painted a dull silver—work harmoniously with the pared-down aesthetic. Roses and hearts romance the intimate corner.

The loft-like open space comprises a small kitchen, living room, and sleeping nook, so creating a harmonious flow was a major consideration. The gray-and white palette and the use of textures rather than patterns produce a smooth and airy union. Subdued pink and blue accents underscore the serene scheme and a glass, iron, and wood theme adds warmth and interest, while natural details bring an organic quality. Sentimental keepsakes keep loved ones ever close. The seasoned furnishings are few but sufficient, simple but cozy. No phone, television, or computer: the only sounds are those of cooing doves, swaying wind chimes, and the faint whistle of a distant train. Peaceful, uncomplicated, and comforting, the barn is my prairie escape—my simpler life.

OPPOSITE Faded pillows convey an unmistakable prairie flair to a bench.

ABOVE A new garden shed is made to look old with whitewashed walls, an old door, and a handmade copper awning.

LEFT More than practical storage, the shed offers shelter for a pair of peace-loving doves who fill the air with their gentle cooing.

CHAPTER 3

VINTAGE PRAIRIE

OPPOSITE, RIGHT AND BELOW Old and new come together in the dining room where pewter, silver, and wood mix with a monochromatic palette. Floating shelves and an oversized sideboard bring a modern touch, while the farmhouse table invites family gatherings. Bouquets in crates, zinc pitchers, and jars impart country accents.

JENNIFER AND ADAM GREY'S HOME MAY BE IN THE CITY, BUT IT IS NO TYPICAL URBAN DWELLING. QUITE THE OPPOSITE, IN FACT.

URBAN PRAIRIE

Though located in a bustling community just outside Los Angeles, California, it is a cozy, up-to-date adaptation of prairie style. But this wasn't the case when the Greys bought the run-down property. "When we first moved in we were eager to get settled and begin this new chapter in our lives, but it quickly became clear that we had to allow the house's potential to unfold," Jennifer recalls. "And sure enough, one by one, each room spoke to us, telling us its needs and wants, from lighting and furnishings to functionality and mood. Getting the old-fashioned farmhouse look I wanted to create

LEFT and OPPOSITE Soft, fluffy cotton bolls gathered in a weathered woven basket and a handwritten note next to a magnolia blossom bring the past and present together eloquently. An old, white wood frame refinished with a dark walnut stain displays a vintage cocoa-bean sack. The inspired repurposing turns the ordinary into art and shows off Jennifer's creative flair.

HOMESPUN FABRICS, WOVEN BASKETS, AND NATURAL ARTIFACTS REDEFINE YESTERDAY'S HISTORY AND INTEGRITY.

was similar to completing a puzzle, with one piece fitting into the next." And with little knowledge of remodeling and a tiny budget but with Adam's energy and the visions dancing in Jennifer's head, the couple turned the derelict city house into their prairie-home dream.

Since she began collecting vintage in her youth, Jennifer always had to surround herself with pieces that make her heart flutter. Her style is ruled by her love affair with nostalgia. "For me, decorating with antiques is a must, much

like breathing," she says. True to her words, she scoured flea markets to find pieces from the past to contribute a timeless feel to her home. Jennifer also has a deep appreciation for aged finishes. "I consider myself a purist," she explains. "I don't see any reason to alter what time has worked so hard to create."

Enlivened with a few pops of color, an earth-tone palette drawn from nature unifies and sustains the rooms' engaging feel and allows the comfortable furnishings to stand on their own

The ingredients of the kitchen mix then and now. Bead
board and glass-fronted cabinets instill a fresh and simple
country mood, echoed by collections of plates, mugs,
and old bowls. An apron sink, a burlap valance, and old
schoolhouse pendant lights pair nicely with the industrial
stools that contribute a contemporary urban farmhouse feel.

A carved fireplace mantel has been fitted with a linen-padded headboard for stylish comfort. Layers of scrumptious blankets in contrasting weights and textures and muted warm tones give the inviting bed a nest-like feel.

merit. Texture plays a vital role as well in setting the comfortable mood and extends a greeting akin to a warm hug. Homespun fabrics, woven baskets, and natural artifacts redefine yesterday's history and integrity. It's a warm and inviting aesthetic with a quietly urban prairie flair that harkens back to a simpler time.

BELOW A day bed layered in white softness and squishy pillows offers a place to read or enjoy a cup of tea. The fabric of the smaller pillow subtly picks up on the opaline hue of the hydrangeas. The little wooden bench and the metal stool's worn finishes add definition to the serene setting.

OPPOSITE Louie cuddles up among vintage comforters stored in an antique basket. An armful of flowers rests on the weathered table in an ephemeral still life—rose, stock, and peony blossoms weave a colorful tapestry and cast their heady fragrance far and wide. A 1954 Chevy truck shows off Lisa's prairie spirit.

PRAIRIE SWEET

WHILE DRIVING AROUND A NEIGHBORHOOD IN THOUSAND OAKS, CALIFORNIA, LISA AND RICH ADKINS HAPPENED ON OLD FARM ROAD, A PICTURESQUE STREET THAT LIVES UP TO ITS NAME, AND, AS FATE WOULD HAVE IT, WITH A HOUSE FOR SALE. "I FELL FOR THE STREET NAME, THE HOUSE, AND THE LOVELY SETTING," LISA SAYS. AND SO IT BEGAN.

Lisa decorates by instinct. "I don't try to make things fit a certain look," she says. "I love what I love." And what she loves is a pretty, comfortable, relaxed style, with furnishings easy to care for, considering her numerous pets have the run of the house. With that in mind, Lisa replaced the existing floor with a durable wood reminiscent of weathered planks that is not only practical but also instills a farmhouse quality throughout the house. The cozy look is made even more cohesive with

MID PLEASURES AND PALACES THOUGH WE MAY ROAM,

BE IT EVER SO HUMBLE, THERE'S NO PLACE LIKE HOME

JOHN EDWARD PAYNE

a quiet palette in calming, fresh colors that provides a luminous backdrop flowing seamlessly throughout the interior.

In Lisa's world, low maintenance and homey also include the beauty of pre-loved furnishings, especially those with layers of peeling paint and rust. Fortunately the area abounds with a plethora of antiques and resale shops and flea markets overflowing with treasures from the past. Lisa gravitates to pieces that show the passage of time

OPPOSITE Aqua appliances and accessories spice up the rusticity of the cabinetry and create a deliberate and cheerful retro feel. Simple lines and natural wood give the island its sturdy farmhouse personality. Flirty chair covers and crochet-trimmed runners provide a feminine touch.

RIGHT Lisa is fond of iron pieces but prefers those with an airy design that bring sculptural elements to enhance her decor and anchor the rooms' clean palette. The fluid lines of the chandelier stand out against the white ceiling. Though imposing, the antique birdcage appears light and weightless positioned against the window, allowing the light through its lace-like wire mesh. The coffee table's battered finish keeps in stride with the pickled pattern of the floor boards. Clarkson finds comfort on a burlap cushion.

Depth and contrast are established through colors, textures, and forms. A pair of carved wood wings, an armoire, and a cast-iron stove anchor the living and dining rooms, gelato-like pastels balance white-clad furnishings, and weathered wood underscores the sweet prairie feel .

A Venetian mirror and rose art introduce
pretty feminine accents. Necessities are
neatly kept out of sight in an old hutch.
Scented lotions, sachets, and lavender make
the bathroom a fragrant and relaxing haven.

but also to simple yet sturdy lines that welcome pets and withstand the demands of daily life. She implements soft touches with fuss-free pretty fabrics that add color, texture, and the occasional floral accents to balance the more rugged aspect of the interior and embrace the ease and charms of prairie style. "I believe that we will be here for ever. I can't imagine loving another home as much as I do this one," Lisa says. "This is our little piece of heaven.... on Old Farm Road."

ABOVE The pristine simplicity of the light-filled bedroom is all about softness and comfort, but tactile linen panels and a rustic bench bring ethereal whites down to earth in allegiance to prairie style.

WHEN IT COMES TO MARIA CARR, IT CAN BE SAID THAT YOU CAN TAKE THE GIRL OUT OF THE PRAIRIE, BUT YOU CAN'T TAKE THE PRAIRIE OUT OF THE GIRL.

INSPIRED PRAIRIE

LEFT AND RIGHT The pastoral setting inspired the interior's fresh palette. Bethany (left) and Nicole help take care of the animals, including a miniature horse, sheep, and bunnies. Boots overflowing with wild flowers and garden blooms stand for romantic prairie. A dainty napkin celebrates the softer side of rustic.

Maria was raised on a dairy farm, aptly named Camas Prairie, in Montana. When she got married, she and her husband Thad moved to Japan, where Thad trained horses. After two years they moved back to a ranch in southern California, and soon after, Thad was offered the management of a horse farm in northern California's magnificent Ione valley. They seized the opportunity to settle in the picturesque hilly landscape with lush meadows and little towns with a history dating back to the early 1800s.

Simple bistro chairs, a farmhouse table, and tree branches masquerading as curtain rods are romanced with a curvy crystal chandelier and flirty airy curtains that add a sense of occasion. Green and blue accents echo the freshness of the outdoors.

ABOVE Old ceiling tiles and a vintage chair wink to yesteryears, while a clock strikes a modern note. The cobalt bucket adds a brilliant splash of color.

At Lost Trail Ranch, the days start early for Maria, Thad, and their five children. By 6 a.m. everybody is tending to the animals in one way or another. "The kids love being part of raising cattle, goats, dogs, horses, and rabbits," Maria says. "It makes for a healthy, rugged outdoor life, which is why our home is all about easy comfort."

RIGHT AND BELOW An old French metal stand with flaking paint and a geometric shape brings a touch of industrial chic. Formerly used for storing vegetables, it now corrals an assortment of the European grain sacks, old mattress ticking, and vintage linens Maria uses to make into the pillows and other home accessories she is creating for Dreamy Whites, her new online business. A lavender soap infuses fabrics with a gentle nostalgic fragrance.

RUGGED FURNISHINGS AND DELICATE FABRICS MELD PRIMITIVE AND PRETTY WITH A KICK-YOUR-BOOTS-OFF STYLE.

The beauty and distinctiveness of Maria's home undeniably reflect the accommodating dual personality of prairie. Rugged furnishings and delicate fabrics meld primitive and pretty with a kick-your-boots-off style. Exquisitely aged pieces in warm pastels come to life against a hushed palette, and barely shielded windows establish the connection with the outside.

Maria first painted all the walls white, then switched a pale gray to add warmth and depth to the rooms. The muted hue makes the mostly white furnishings more welcoming, and green and blue accents blend in rather than stand out.

Potted herbs make a fragrant and organic centerpiece. The contemporary light pendant and the crystal chandelier perpetuate the yin-yang look that characterizes every room.

OPPOSITE LEFT AND RIGHT Aqua spatterware and a burlap runner combine color and texture. The old-fashioned armoire is the epitome of prairie charm, displaying a collection of ironstone and galvanized pitchers.

Maria has always favored
handmade antiques, not for their
pedigree but for the significance of
their past, and through the process
of decorating her new home also
developed an attachment for the
feel of the Provençal farmhouse
interiors and vintage linens. "Both
are unpretentious and beautiful in
their simplicity," she says. However,
she admits to being seduced by
a few elegant touches. "Crystal
chandeliers are my Achilles' heel",
she says, "particularly when they

MAY THE SUN BRING YOU NEW ENERGY BY DAY, MAY THE MOON
SOFTLY RESTORE YOU BY NIGHT,

MAY YOU WALK GENTLY THROUGH THE WORLD AND KNOW ITS
BEAUTY ALL THE DAYS OF YOUR LIFE.

APACHE BLESSING

Green accents and a shy touch of pink give the guest room its oh-so-fresh attitude. The mantel offers a spot of choice for a trio of Mason jars filled with clusters of blushing roses. The shade of the pink alabaster bedside lamp is dressed in an antique fabric remnant edged with a rosy border. Decorative and functional, the cowboy hats are put to good use every day.

Simply but comfortably furnished, the bedroom personifies the coveted prairie look. Pillow cases fashioned from vintage grain sacks complement the rustic, weathered-door headboard and bistro chairs, while the chandelier, bed linens, and gauzy curtains send ripples of romance. Painted white, an old coal bucket is a striking container for garden-fresh hydrangeas in the perfect hues of greens and blues. The cowboy hat makes a lighthearted lampshade.

LEFT AND OPPOSITE The poetry of the prairie lives on into the night. Cloaked in a velvet sky, a simple setting among shadowy oaks and wild grasses shimmers under the silver moon. Creatures large and small are an endearing part of the landscape. A prettily dressed picnic table awaits the children with an offering of cherries and homemade lemonade. A basket of fresh picked apples was meant to be shared. but Dolly the goat could not resist!

are mixed with something rustic." Throughout the house several sparkling examples next to architectural salvage attest eloquently, and stylishly, to her weakness for the endearing mix. As for antique textiles, she prefers those that show the irregularities and subtleties found in old French linens and European grain sacks, which, with the help of her mother and sisters, Trudy and Elizabeth, are made into pillows, throws, and table runners.

Though Maria gave up her dream of becoming an artist in favor of taking care of her growing family, in the end, as her home and her healthy, happy brood prove, she successfully accomplishes both. "I don't think we could find a better place to raise our children," she says. "They thrive in this environment. Thad gets to do what he loves, and I am turning my passions into a new venture. Life here is blissfully simple."

OPPOSITE Rustic meets romance in this seductive outdoor room meant for daydreaming and balmy summer evenings. Intimate meals as well as family gatherings are enjoyed on the deck. Gently rusted and worn furnishings and mismatched dinnerware and accessories embrace the simplicity of outdoor life with gusto and charm.

RIGHT More than a collection, vintage clocks are reminders of the value of time. A hammock beckons with the unaffected coziness of contrasting warm woolen and fresh florals.

RUSTIC PRAIRIE

ONCE UPON A TIME, HIGH IN THE RUGGED MOUNTAINS OF THE NORTHERN CALIFORNIA SIERRAS, A HUMBLE ONE-BEDROOM WOODEN CABIN WAS HOME TO A FAMILY OF HOPEFUL SETTLERS. Nearly a century later, Michelle and Scott McCauley traveled along the narrow road that winds up a steep bluff through towering spruces, leading the way to that very same cabin.

Though it lacked the standard amenities, and its 600 square feet could hardly accommodate their family of four, the cabin's rough but charmingly rustic appearance and idyllic setting were the answer to their quest for a simpler life. They knew for certain that with their shared talents—Scott is a contractor and Michelle owns an antique store—they could make it their own. Their goal was to keep the mood and feel intact. As Michelle says,

The small living room is big on comfort. Mirrors amplify both the natural light and the space. In lieu of a space-gobbling fireplace, a stocky Jotul wood-burning stove with a slate backing provides welcoming warmth during the winter. The sparkling chandelier adds a touch of luxury.

ABOVE Rustic hooks on weathered boards are used to hang flower-filled jars in summer and coats, hats, scarves, and wet gloves in winter. Boots are the right fit for the rugged outdoors.

TOP LEFT Overflowing with lush garden roses, an old enamel coffee pot and a dainty teacup and saucer are elegant and timeless grace notes.

BOTTOM LEFT Rustic meets refined in this charmingly worn old shelf paired with some of Michelle's inherited collection of fine china.

ABOVE A floral panel conceals storage and softens the cupboards' aged finish. Ironstone pitchers and Mason jars make pretty and practical catchalls.

OPPOSITE The dining room centers around a family-size table flanked by long benches offering plenty of seating. Plain cabinets fronted with old bead board look as they have always belonged.

"Our mantra was recycle, reinvent, reuse." To that end, Scott added a bedroom and bathroom with wood acquired from barns slated for demolition, old redwood planks salvaged from remodeling jobs, and vintage doors and windows rescued from the wrecker's ball that complement the indigenous hand-hewn materials from which the woody cabin was initially constructed.

Inside and out, rugged furnishings, natural wood, worn surfaces, and simple lines communicate the cabin's origin without precluding comfort and charm. Cushy fabrics, plump pillows, weathered pieces, and homely accents offset the rusticity inherent in the rooms and reflect Michelle's

A generous sideboard provides stylish storage for resilient restaurant ware and ironstone, while a small cupboard is reserved for more delicate collections.

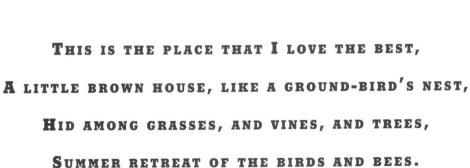

THIS IS THE PLACE THAT I LOVE THE BEST,

A LITTLE BROWN HOUSE, LIKE A GROUND-BIRD'S NEST,

HID AMONG GRASSES, AND VINES, AND TREES,

SUMMER RETREAT OF THE BIRDS AND BEES.

ELLA WHEELER WILCOX

ABOVE AND LEFT Fresh roses and old books create a lovely still life. A creamy palette, warm floral accents, and a pleasing mix of textiles contribute romantic undertones to the new bedroom. The floor is kept bare to expose the raw beauty of the wood and help maintain a link to the original cabin.

OPPOSITE LEFT A fireplace mantel turned headboard offers a shelf for vintage paintings that share the linens' patterns and hues.

OPPOSITE RIGHT Reminiscent of the old days, a quaint medicine cabinet and a dresser shelter necessities.

romantic touches. In the living room, an heirloom chandelier gently sparkles next to an old wood-burning stove, while pillows, bedcovers, and paintings with pretty floral accents soften the bedroom.

In celebrating the spirit of the century-old cabin and respecting its authenticity, Michelle and Scott not only preserved the past and made their dream of a simpler life a reality, but also got the rustic prairie look just right.

penchants and passions. Her idea of "roughing it" includes mixing fine china with local pottery and vintage fabrics and wooly blankets. Regional antiques and castoffs gleaned from friends, family, and Michelle's own store are also much in evidence.

"Staying true to the cabin and the times dictated how it should be furnished," Michelle explains. "But it was equally as important for everything to be meaningful and have a purpose." The same principle is applied to everyday items: durable, useful ironstone shares space with a treasured family silver tea set, and Mason jars replace standard drinking glasses

Keeping within the decorating boundaries Michelle implemented doesn't exclude a few

ABOVE Impervious to weather changes, a robust old ice box remains a constant feature and offers a fittingly rustic sideboard and convenient storage.

RIGHT Douglas fir, hemlock, and incense cedar cradle the picturesque cabin in a fragrant embrace. Candles illuminate the night and cast a golden glow that radiates warmth and alludes to the home's humble beginnings. The original wood shingles and siding inspired the new covered front entry and bedroom, to the left, preserving the integrity of the original architecture and rough-hewn character of the cabin. The aqua shutters and door add lively accents.